IT'S THE END OF THE WORLD!

ASTEROID IMPACT

BY LISA OWINGS

TORQUE™

BELLWETHER MEDIA • MINNEAPOLIS, MN

Are you ready to take it to the extreme? Torque books thrust you into the action-packed world of sports, vehicles, mystery, and adventure. These books may include dirt, smoke, fire, and chilling tales.
WARNING: read at your own risk.

This edition first published in 2020 by Bellwether Media, Inc.

No part of this publication may be reproduced in whole or in part without written permission of the publisher.
For information regarding permission, write to Bellwether Media, Inc., Attention: Permissions Department,
6012 Blue Circle Drive, Minnetonka, MN 55343.

Library of Congress Cataloging-in-Publication Data

Names: Owings, Lisa, author.
Title: Asteroid Impact / by Lisa Owings.
Description: Minneapolis, MN : Bellwether Media, Inc., [2020] | Series: Torque: It's the End of the World! | Audience: Ages 7-12. | Audience: Grades 3 to 7. | Includes bibliographical references and index.
Identifiers: LCCN 2019000972 (print) | LCCN 2019006428 (ebook) | ISBN 9781618916518 (ebook) | ISBN 9781644870792 (hardcover : alk. paper)
Subjects: LCSH: Asteroids–Collisions with Earth–Juvenile literature. | Near-earth asteroids–Juvenile literature. | Extinction (Biology)–Juvenile literature.
Classification: LCC QB377 (ebook) | LCC QB377 .0945 2020 (print) | DDC 523.44–dc23
LC record available at https://lccn.loc.gov/2019000972

Text copyright © 2020 by Bellwether Media, Inc. TORQUE and associated logos are trademarks and/or registered trademarks of Bellwether Media, Inc. SCHOLASTIC, CHILDREN'S PRESS, and associated logos are trademarks and/or registered trademarks of Scholastic Inc., 557 Broadway, New York, NY 10012.

Editor: Rebecca Sabelko   Designer: Andrea Schneider

Printed in the United States of America, North Mankato, MN.

TABLE OF CONTENTS

BRACE FOR IMPACT!	4
A MAJOR HIT	8
ASTEROIDS ON THE LOOSE	12
NOT IN OUR LIFETIME	18
GLOSSARY	22
TO LEARN MORE	23
INDEX	24

BRACE FOR IMPACT!

The world's best scientists have failed to stop the asteroid. There was hope for a few years. Then came the **evacuations**. People tunneled like moles. Your family settled in an underground city. You have enough supplies for a year or two.

Today everything changes. You stand in the sunshine as long as you can. Then your parents call you down to the shelter.

⚠️ TALKING SHELTER

Many mammals survived the blast that killed the dinosaurs by burrowing underground. The same plan may work for people.

The countdown to impact blares from the radio. Just a few more minutes now. You wonder if you will feel it.

Soon everything goes dark and silent. Then the ground starts shaking. The noise becomes almost deafening. You close your eyes and hug your family close. All you can do now is wait.

A MAJOR HIT

Asteroids are space rocks left behind after the solar system formed. Like planets, they **orbit** the Sun. But once in a while, one zooms toward Earth. What would happen if it hit our planet?

The large asteroid slams into Earth like a **nuclear bomb**! Flaming rock rains from the skies. Cities crumble from **earthquakes** and **tsunamis**. Lava and ash spew from **volcanoes**. Finally, a cloud of dust blocks out the sun.

IMPACT WINTER

A large asteroid would kick up enough dust to block out the sun. This could cause a long impact winter with dark, cold weather. Plants would die, making food scarce.

The last deadly asteroid hit 65 million years ago. Many scientists believe the impact led to the end of the dinosaurs. It is possible another deadly asteroid could smash into Earth.

CHAIN REACTION

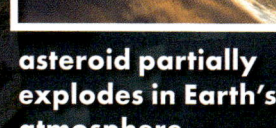

asteroid partially explodes in Earth's atmosphere

flaming rocks rain from the sky

natural disasters destroy cities

impact winter causes temperatures to drop and life to struggle

Scientists are working to protect the planet. If they fail, governments will order evacuations and build shelters. Plants will die. Survivors will fail to find food. Life on Earth will hang in the balance.

ASTEROIDS ON THE LOOSE

Space objects have long been a source of fear. The first asteroids were spotted in the early 1800s. Scientists later learned that asteroids sometimes hit planets.

ASTEROID

A LOOK BACK:
THE CHELYABINSK ASTEROID

FEBRUARY 15, 2013

CHELYABINSK, RUSSIA

A blinding light streaked through the sky. Then a house-sized asteroid exploded in the air. The blast shattered glass all over the city. Over 1,600 people were hurt. Most were struck by broken glass. Many others were burned or briefly blinded.

Scientist Luis Alvarez wanted to know why the dinosaurs disappeared. In 1980, he reported that a huge asteroid may have been the cause. This showed an asteroid could put all life on Earth in danger.

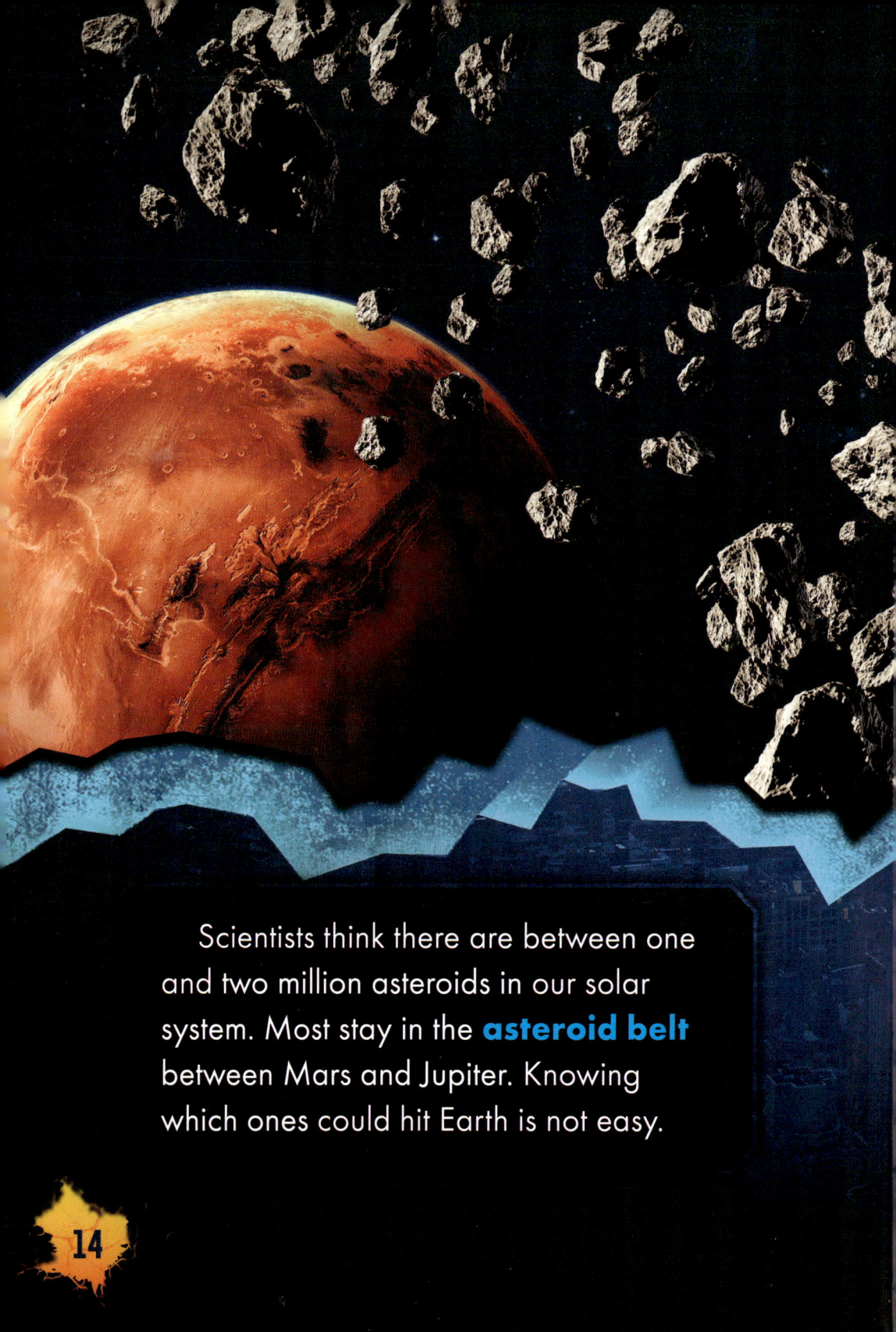

Scientists think there are between one and two million asteroids in our solar system. Most stay in the **asteroid belt** between Mars and Jupiter. Knowing which ones could hit Earth is not easy.

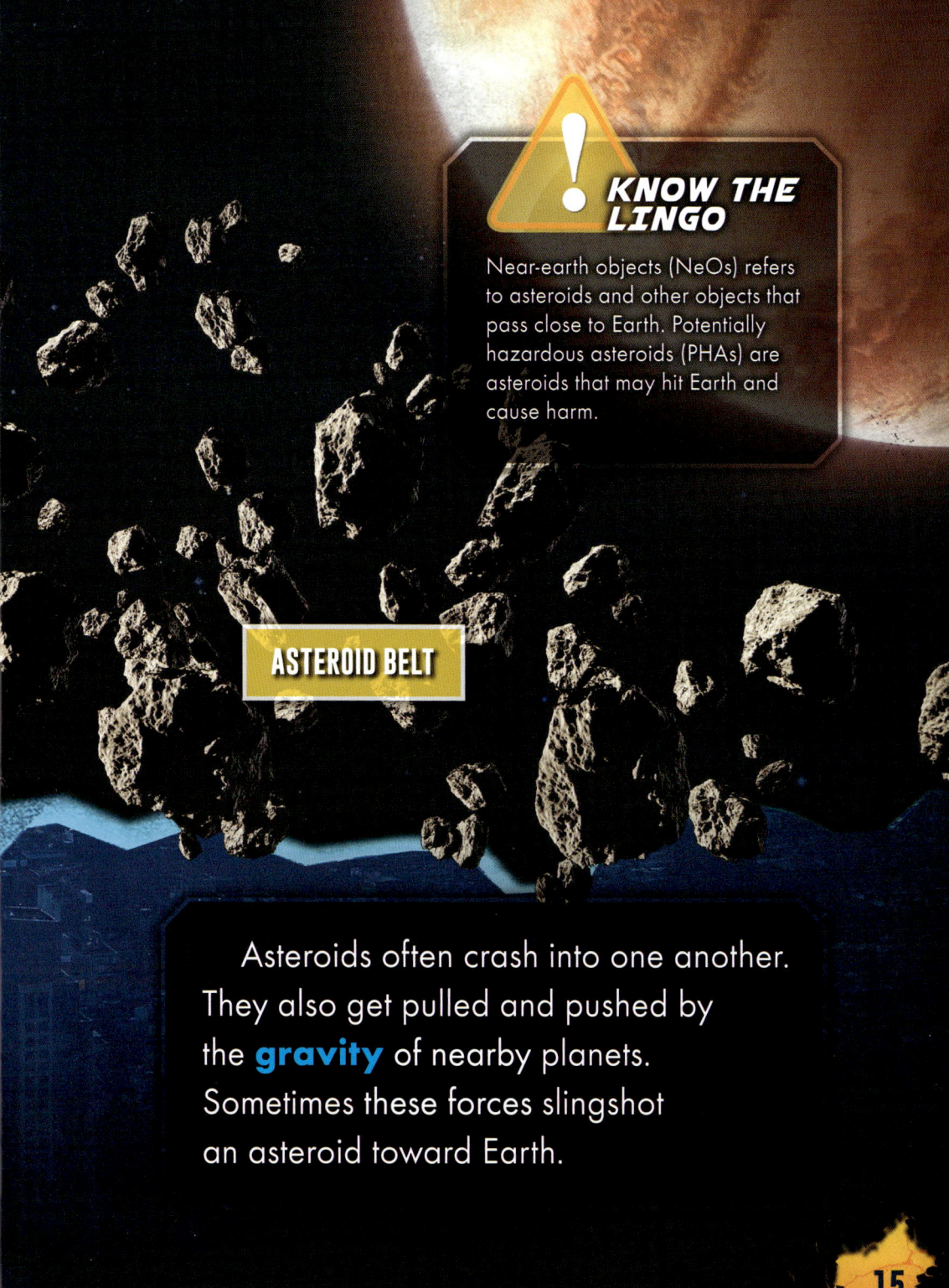

⚠ KNOW THE LINGO

Near-earth objects (NeOs) refers to asteroids and other objects that pass close to Earth. Potentially hazardous asteroids (PHAs) are asteroids that may hit Earth and cause harm.

ASTEROID BELT

Asteroids often crash into one another. They also get pulled and pushed by the **gravity** of nearby planets. Sometimes these forces slingshot an asteroid toward Earth.

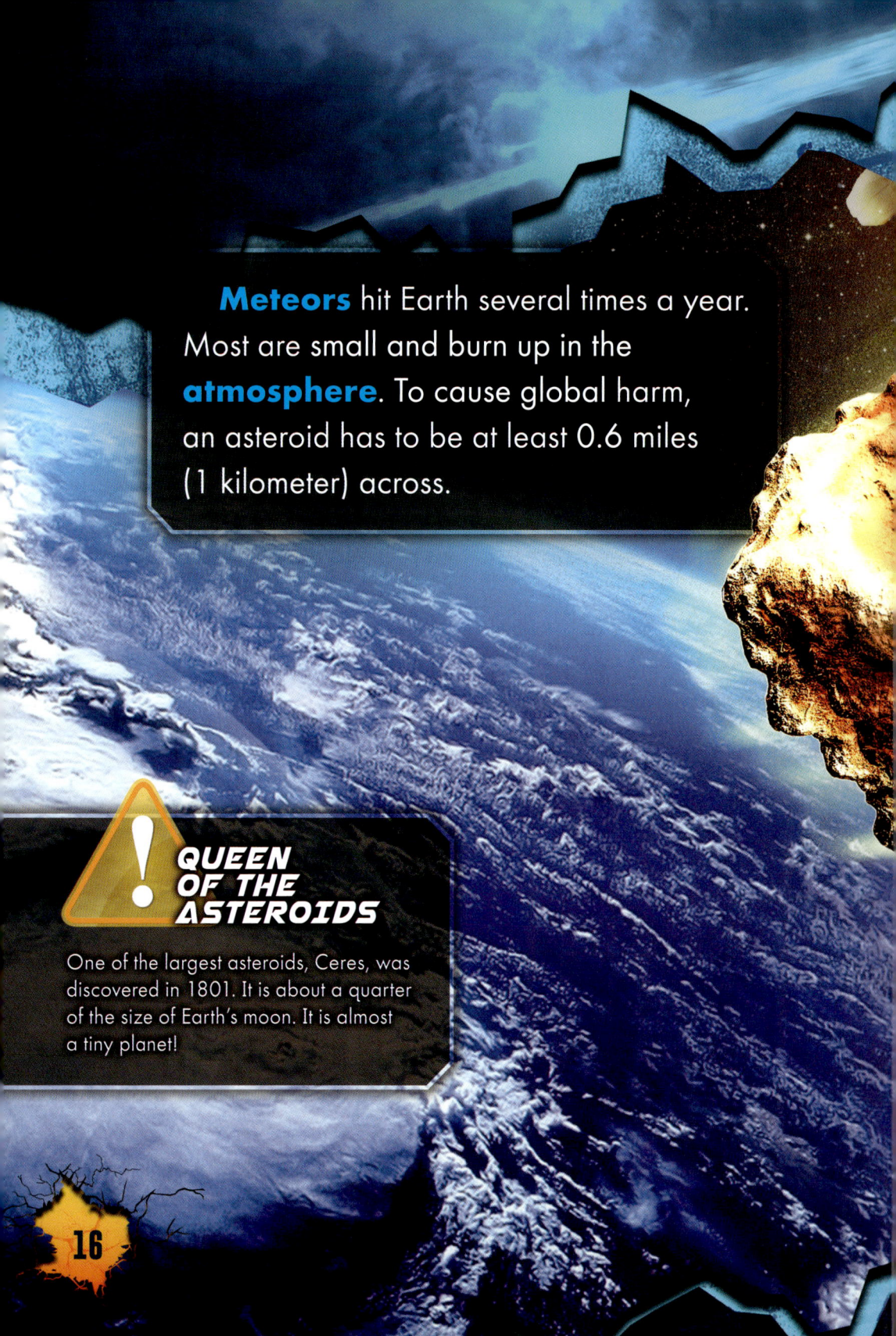

Meteors hit Earth several times a year. Most are small and burn up in the **atmosphere**. To cause global harm, an asteroid has to be at least 0.6 miles (1 kilometer) across.

QUEEN OF THE ASTEROIDS

One of the largest asteroids, Ceres, was discovered in 1801. It is about a quarter of the size of Earth's moon. It is almost a tiny planet!

An impact by an asteroid of this size would be deadlier than the most powerful bomb. **Natural disasters** and **climate** changes would follow. Nearly all life on Earth could disappear!

NOT IN OUR LIFETIME

Scientists use **telescopes** to find and track asteroids. Computer **simulations** show the risk of impact.

No deadly asteroids are due to hit Earth for at least the next hundred years. Asteroids like the one that led to the death of the dinosaurs come around once every hundred million years or so.

MISSION TO BENNU

In 2016, NASA launched mission OSIRIS-REx. They sent the spacecraft to the asteroid Bennu. The craft will bring back a rock sample to study in 2023. Bennu has a small chance of hitting Earth between 2175 and 2199.

IN THE MEDIA
BOOK TITLE:
LIFE AS WE KNEW IT
AUTHOR:
SUSAN BETH PFEFFER
YEAR RELEASED: 2008

About the book: An asteroid strikes the Moon and knocks it closer to Earth. Miranda and her family prepare for natural disasters. They know the world may come to an end.

Could it happen?: The Moon could only be moved by an asteroid its same size. It would likely shatter. Earth would not survive.

Scientists are studying ways to move asteroids out of Earth's path. They could fly a **gravity tractor** near an asteroid to tug it off course. Bumping an asteroid with a spacecraft or setting off a bomb near it are other ideas.

The next world-ending asteroid is millions of years away. By the time it comes, we will have a great chance of defending Earth!

GLOSSARY

asteroid belt—a part of space between Mars and Jupiter where many asteroids orbit the sun

atmosphere—the gases that surround Earth

climate—the average weather of a place over a long period of time

earthquakes—shakings of the Earth's surface that often cause a lot of damage

evacuations—moving away from dangerous areas

gravity—the force that pulls objects toward one another

gravity tractor—a large spacecraft that would fly near an asteroid and pull it off course

meteors—pieces of rock or metal from space that leave bright trails as they pass through Earth's atmosphere

natural disasters—sudden events in nature that cause great harm

nuclear bomb—the most dangerous weapon on Earth

orbit—to move around something in a fixed path

simulations—computer models of objects or events that are often hard or dangerous to study in real life

telescopes—devices used for seeing distant objects, especially those in outer space

tsunamis—powerful waves caused by an underwater earthquake

volcanoes—holes in the earth; when a volcano erupts, hot ash, gas, or melted rock called lava shoots out.

TO LEARN MORE

AT THE LIBRARY

Kukla, Lauren. *Asteroids, Comets, and Meteoroids*. Minneapolis, Minn.: ABDO Publishing, 2017.

Peterson, Megan Cooley. *The Dinosaur Extinction: What Really Happened?* Mankato, Minn.: Black Rabbit Books, 2019.

Rusch, Elizabeth. *Impact! Asteroids and the Science of Saving the World*. Boston, Mass.: Houghton Mifflin Harcourt, 2017.

ON THE WEB

FACTSURFER

Factsurfer.com gives you a safe, fun way to find more information.

1. Go to www.factsurfer.com
2. Enter "asteroid impact" into the search box and click 🔍.
3. Select your book cover to see a list of related web sites.

INDEX

Alvarez, Luis, 13
asteroid belt, 14, 15
atmosphere, 16
Bennu, 19
Ceres, 16
chain reaction, 11
Chelyabinsk asteroid, 13
computer simulations, 18
dinosaurs, 5, 10, 13, 18
Earth, 8, 10, 11, 13, 14, 15, 16, 17, 18, 19, 21
evacuations, 4, 11
food, 9, 11
governments, 11
gravity, 15
gravity tractor, 21
impact winter, 9
life, 11, 13, 17

Life as We Knew It, 20
meteors, 16
natural disasters, 8, 17
orbit, 8
OSIRIS-REx, 19
planets, 8, 11, 12, 14, 15, 16
scientists, 4, 10, 11, 12, 13, 14, 18, 21
shelter, 4, 11
solar system, 8, 14
space rocks, 8, 12, 15, 19
spacecraft, 19, 21
Sun, 4, 8, 9
supplies, 4, 6
survivors, 11
telescopes, 18

The images in this book are reproduced through the courtesy of: onepup, front cover (city before); Alones, front cover, pp. 2-3, 20-21 (city after); IgorZh, front cover, pp. 2-3, 20-21 (asteroids); alexandralarina, p. 5 (boy); ChameleonsEye, pp. 4-5 (well); Africa Studio, p. 6 (mom and boy); Tunatura, p. 7 (girl); Sementer, pp. 6-7 (tunnel); Zastolskiy Victor, pp. 8-9; Herschel Hoffmeyer, pp. 10 (T-rex, triceratops), 10-11 (background); The7Dew, p. 10 (asteroid); muratart, p. 11 (top left); Tanguy de Saint-Cry, p. 11 (bottom left); Triff, p. 11 (top right); Markus Gann, p. 11 (bottom right); 3000ad, pp. 12-13 (asteroid); sripfoto, pp. 12-13 (Milky Way); Alex Alishevskikh/ Wiki Commons, p. 13 (Chelyabinsk asteroid); Vadiim SAdovski, pp. 14 (Mars), 15 (Jupiter); klss, pp. 14-15 (asteroid belt); Oliver Denker, pp. 16-17; FrameStockFootages, pp. 18-19; NASA Images, p. 19 (OSIRIS-REx); Wikipedia, p. 20 (book cover); Dotted Yeti, p. 21 (gravity tractor).